FAVORITE BRAND NAME  RECIPES™

DINER
RECIPES

Publications International, Ltd.

Pictured on the back cover *(left to right):* Greek Isles Omelet *(page 4)* and Grilled Reuben Burger *(page 72).*

ISBN: 978-1-68022-500-6

Library of Congress Control Number: 2016939495

Manufactured in China.

8 7 6 5 4 3 2 1

Microwave Cooking: Microwave ovens vary in wattage. Use the cooking times as guidelines and check for doneness before adding more time.

Preparation/Cooking Times: Preparation times are based on the approximate amount of time required to assemble the recipe before cooking, baking, chilling or serving. These times include preparation steps such as measuring, chopping and mixing. The fact that some preparations and cooking can be done simultaneously is taken into account. Preparation of optional ingredients and serving suggestions is not included.

TABLE OF CONTENTS

ALL-DAY BREAKFAST

GREEK ISLES OMELET
MAKES 2 SERVINGS

1 tablespoon olive oil, divided

¼ cup chopped onion

¼ cup canned artichoke hearts, rinsed and drained

¼ cup chopped spinach

¼ cup chopped plum tomato

2 tablespoons sliced pitted black olives, rinsed and drained

4 eggs

Dash black pepper

1 Heat 2 teapoons oil in small nonstick skillet over medium heat. Add onion; cook and stir 2 minutes or until crisp-tender. Add artichokes; cook and stir until heated through. Add spinach, tomato and olives; gently stir until blended. Transfer to small bowl.

2 Wipe out skillet with paper towels. Heat remaining 1 teaspoon oil over medium heat. Whisk eggs and pepper in medium bowl until well blended. Pour egg mixture into skillet; cook and stir gently, lifting edge to allow uncooked portion to flow underneath. Continue cooking just until set.

3 Spoon vegetable mixture over half of omelet; gently loosen omelet with spatula and fold in half. Serve immediately.

SKILLET SAUSAGE WITH POTATOES AND ROSEMARY

MAKES 4 TO 6 SERVINGS

1 tablespoon vegetable oil

3 cups diced red skin potatoes

1 cup diced onion

1 pound BOB EVANS® Original Recipe Roll Sausage

½ teaspoon dried rosemary

¼ teaspoon rubbed sage

Salt and black pepper to taste

2 tablespoons chopped fresh parsley

Heat oil in large skillet over medium-high heat 1 minute. Add potatoes; cook 5 to 10 minutes or until slightly brown, stirring occasionally. Add onion; cook until tender. Add crumbled sausage; cook until browned. Add rosemary, sage, salt and pepper; cook and stir until well blended. Transfer to serving platter and garnish with parsley. Refrigerate leftovers.

SPINACH, TOMATO AND HAM SCRAMBLE

MAKES 4 SERVINGS

SALSA

½ cup cherry tomatoes, diced

1 medium jalapeño pepper,* seeded and finely chopped

1 tablespoon finely chopped red onion

1 tablespoon chopped fresh cilantro

1 tablespoon lime juice

⅛ teaspoon salt

Jalapeño peppers can sting and irritate the skin, so wear rubber gloves when handling peppers and do not touch your eyes.

SCRAMBLE

8 eggs

¼ cup milk

1 tablespoon butter

3 ounces diced ham

½ cup (1 ounce) baby spinach, coarsely chopped

½ cup cherry tomatoes, quartered

¼ cup sour cream

4 lime wedges

1 Combine salsa ingredients in small bowl; mix well.

2 Whisk eggs and milk in small bowl until well blended. Melt butter in large nonstick skillet over medium heat. Add egg mixture; cook 3 minutes or until almost set. Gently fold in ham, spinach and tomatoes; cook 1 minute.

3 Top each serving with salsa and sour cream. Serve with lime wedges.

ALL-DAY BREAKFAST

BANANA-NUT
BUTTERMILK WAFFLES
MAKES 4 SERVINGS

¾ cup walnuts or pecans, plus additional for garnish

2 cups all-purpose flour

¼ cup sugar

2 teaspoons baking powder

1 teaspoon salt

2 eggs, separated

2 cups buttermilk

2 very ripe bananas, mashed (about 1 cup)

¼ cup (½ stick) butter, melted

1 teaspoon vanilla

Maple syrup and banana slices

1 Toast ¾ cup walnuts in medium skillet over medium heat 5 minutes or until fragrant, stirring frequently. Transfer to plate; chop walnuts when cool.

2 Lightly spray waffle iron with nonstick cooking spray; preheat according to manufacturer's directions.

3 Meanwhile, combine flour, sugar, baking powder and salt in large bowl; mix well. Beat egg yolks in medium bowl. Add buttermilk, mashed bananas, butter, vanilla and toasted walnuts; stir until well blended. Add to flour mixture; stir just until moistened.

4 Beat egg whites in medium bowl with electric mixer at high speed until stiff but not dry. Fold egg whites into batter.

5 Pour ¾ cup batter into waffle iron; bake 4 to 6 minutes or until golden brown. Repeat with remaining batter. Serve with maple syrup and banana slices; garnish with additional walnuts.

ALL-DAY BREAKFAST

EASY EGGS BENEDICT

MAKES 4 SERVINGS

¼ cup white vinegar

1 teaspoon salt

4 English muffins, split

4 tablespoons (½ stick) butter, softened, divided

8 slices Canadian bacon

8 eggs

1 can (6 ounces) hollandaise sauce

Pinch ground red pepper

1 Preheat oven to 170°F. Fill large saucepan with about 2 quarts water; bring to a boil over high heat. Add vinegar and salt; reduce heat to a simmer. While water is heating, toast English muffin halves; spread toasted muffin halves with 2 tablespoons butter. Place muffin halves on ovenproof platter.

2 Place bacon on microwavable plate; microwave on HIGH about 15 seconds or just until warm. Place 1 slice bacon on each toasted muffin half. Place platter in oven to keep warm.

3 To poach eggs, crack 1 egg into small bowl. Gently drop egg into simmering water. Repeat with another egg. Use wooden spoon to move eggs gently to keep from sticking to bottom of saucepan. Simmer 2 to 3 minutes or until egg white is cooked through. Remove poached eggs with slotted spoon; place in shallow pie plate or baking dish. Trim any ragged edges to make circular shape. Repeat, cooking 2 eggs at a time, until all eggs are poached. Remove bacon-topped muffin halves from oven. Place 2 halves on each plate; place 1 egg on each muffin half.

4 Heat hollandaise sauce in small saucepan over low heat or in microwave 1 to 2 minutes or just until warm, stirring frequently. *Do not boil.* Stir in remaining 2 tablespoons butter and red pepper until butter is melted and mixture is smooth and well blended. Spoon warm hollandaise over each egg.

NOTE

Some markets sell hollandaise sauce mixes in 1.25-ounce packages instead of cans. Follow the package directions, omitting the 2 tablespoons butter; stir in red pepper.

TIP

If necessary, reheat the poached eggs before serving. Gently slip them into the hot water and let stand about 20 seconds.

ALL-DAY BREAKFAST

SAWMILL BISCUITS AND GRAVY

MAKES 8 SERVINGS

3 tablespoons canola or vegetable oil, divided

8 ounces bulk breakfast sausage

2¼ cups plus 3 tablespoons biscuit baking mix, divided

2⅔ cups whole milk, divided

¼ teaspoon salt or to taste

¼ teaspoon black pepper or to taste

1 Preheat oven to 450°F. Heat 1 tablespoon oil in large nonstick skillet over medium heat. Add sausage; cook and stir until browned, breaking up larger pieces. Remove to plate with slotted spoon.

2 Add remaining 2 tablespoons oil to skillet. Add 3 tablespoons baking mix; whisk until smooth. Gradually add 2 cups milk; cook and stir 3 to 4 minutes or until mixture comes to a boil. Cook 1 minute or until thickened, stirring constantly. Add sausage and any accumulated juices; cook and stir 2 minutes. Season with salt and pepper.

3 Combine remaining 2¼ cups biscuit mix and ⅔ cup milk in medium bowl; mix well. Spoon batter into 8 mounds onto ungreased nonstick baking sheet.

4 Bake 8 to 10 minutes or until golden. Serve warm with gravy.

HAM AND VEGETABLE OMELET

MAKES 4 SERVINGS

1 tablespoon butter, divided

2 ounces (about ½ cup) diced ham

1 small onion, diced

½ medium green bell pepper, diced

½ medium red bell pepper, diced

2 cloves garlic, minced

6 eggs, beaten

⅛ teaspoon black pepper

½ cup (2 ounces) shredded Colby cheese, divided

1 medium tomato, chopped

Hot pepper sauce (optional)

1 Melt 2 teaspoons butter in large nonstick skillet over medium-high heat. Add ham, onion, bell peppers and garlic; cook and stir 5 minutes or until vegetables are crisp-tender. Transfer to large bowl.

2 Wipe out skillet with paper towels. Melt remaining 1 teaspoon butter over medium-high heat. Pour eggs into skillet; sprinkle with black pepper. Cook about 2 minutes or until bottom is set, lifting edges with spatula to allow uncooked portion to flow underneath. Reduce heat to medium-low; cover and cook 4 minutes or until top is set.

3 Gently slide omelet onto large serving plate; spoon ham mixture down center. Sprinkle with ¼ cup cheese. Carefully fold 2 sides of omelet over ham mixture; sprinkle with remaining ¼ cup cheese and tomato. Cut into 4 wedges; serve immediately with hot pepper sauce, if desired.

APPLE PANCAKES

MAKES 10 TO 12 PANCAKES

2 tablespoons plus
2 teaspoons butter

1¼ cups milk

1 egg, beaten

1 cup all-purpose flour

¼ cup whole wheat flour

¼ cup finely chopped
dried apple

¼ cup golden raisins or
chopped pecans

3 tablespoons sugar

1 tablespoon baking
powder

1 teaspoon ground
cinnamon

½ teaspoon salt

Maple syrup

1 Melt butter in large skillet or griddle over medium heat. Pour
into medium bowl, leaving thin film of butter on skillet. Add
milk and egg to bowl; whisk until blended.

2 Combine all-purpose flour, whole wheat flour, apple, raisins,
sugar, baking powder, cinnamon and salt in large bowl; mix
well. Add milk mixture; stir just until blended. *Do not beat.*

3 Pour batter by ¼ cupfuls into skillet. Cook over medium heat
2 to 3 minutes per side or until golden brown. Serve with
maple syrup.

GOLDEN SUNRISE FRENCH TOAST

MAKES 4 TO 5 SERVINGS | PREP TIME 10 MINUTES **COOK TIME** 10 MINUTES

2 large eggs

1 can (12 fluid ounces)
NESTLÉ® CARNATION®
Evaporated Lowfat
2% Milk

2 teaspoons vanilla extract

2 tablespoons granulated
sugar

1 tablespoon *plus*
1½ teaspoons
all-purpose flour

¼ teaspoon salt

8 to 10 slices (¾-inch-thick)
firm, day-old French
bread

Unsalted butter

Maple syrup

Fresh seasonal berries
or sliced fruit

HEAT large skillet over medium heat for 3 to 4 minutes.

BEAT eggs in shallow pan or large pie plate; whisk in evaporated milk and vanilla extract. Whisk in sugar, flour and salt. Add several slices of bread; soak without oversaturating.

SWIRL 1 tablespoon butter in hot skillet. Remove bread from batter, allowing excess batter to drip off; transfer prepared bread to skillet in single layer. Cook for 2 minutes or until golden brown. Turn over; cook for an additional 2 minutes or until golden. Serve immediately with syrup and berries. Continue with remaining bread slices, adding 1 tablespoon butter to skillet for each new batch.

BACON-CHEESE GRITS

MAKES 4 SERVINGS

2 cups milk

½ cup quick-cooking grits

1½ cups (6 ounces) shredded sharp Cheddar cheese *or* 6 slices American cheese, torn into bite-size pieces

2 tablespoons butter

1 teaspoon Worcestershire sauce

½ teaspoon salt

⅛ teaspoon ground red pepper (optional)

4 thick-cut slices bacon, crisp-cooked and chopped

1 Bring milk to a boil in large saucepan over medium-high heat. Slowly stir in grits; return to a boil. Reduce heat to low; cover and simmer 5 minutes, stirring frequently.

2 Remove from heat; stir in cheese, butter, Worcestershire sauce, salt and red pepper, if desired. Cover and let stand 2 minutes or until cheese melts. Top with bacon.

VARIATION

For a thinner consistency, add an additional ½ cup milk.

SUNNY DAY BREAKFAST BURRITOS

MAKES 4 SERVINGS

1 tablespoon butter

½ cup chopped red or green bell pepper

2 green onions, sliced

6 eggs

2 tablespoons milk

¼ teaspoon salt

4 (7-inch) flour tortillas, warmed

½ cup shredded colby jack or Mexican cheese blend

½ cup salsa

1 Melt butter in medium skillet over medium heat. Add bell pepper and green onions; cook and stir about 3 minutes or until vegetables are softened.

2 Whisk eggs, milk and salt in medium bowl until blended. Pour mixture into skillet. Reduce heat to low; cook until eggs are just set, stirring gently. (Eggs should be soft with no liquid remaining.)

3 Spoon one fourth of egg mixture down center of each tortilla; top with 2 tablespoons cheese. Fold in sides of tortillas to enclose filling. Serve with salsa.

CORNED BEEF HASH

MAKES 4 SERVINGS

2 large russet potatoes, peeled and cut into ½-inch cubes

½ teaspoon salt

¼ teaspoon black pepper

¼ cup (½ stick) butter

1 cup chopped onion

½ pound corned beef, finely chopped

1 tablespoon horseradish

4 eggs

1 Place potatoes in large skillet; add water to cover. Bring to a boil over high heat. Reduce heat to low; cook 6 minutes. (Potatoes will be firm.) Remove potatoes from skillet; drain well. Sprinkle with salt and pepper.

2 Melt butter in same skillet over medium heat. Add onion; cook and stir 5 minutes. Add corned beef, horseradish and potatoes; mix well. Press mixture with spatula to flatten.

3 Reduce heat to low; cook 10 to 15 minutes. Turn hash in large pieces; pat down and cook 10 to 15 minutes or until bottom is well browned.

4 Meanwhile, bring 1 inch of water to a simmer in small saucepan. Break one egg into shallow dish; carefully slide into water. Cook 5 minutes or until white is opaque. Remove with slotted spoon to plate; keep warm. Repeat with remaining eggs.

5 Top each serving of hash with 1 egg. Serve immediately.

SOUPS & SALADS

TOMATO VEGETABLE SOUP

MAKES 10 SERVINGS | PREP TIME 10 MINUTES **COOK TIME** 45 MINUTES

1 bottle (64 fluid ounces) CAMPBELL'S® Tomato Juice

1 clove garlic, minced

¼ teaspoon *each* ground black pepper, dried thyme and basil leaves, crushed

1 bag (16 ounces) frozen Italian-style mixed vegetables

1 package (16 ounces) frozen succotash

¾ cup chopped Vidalia onion

1 Heat the juice, garlic, black pepper, thyme, basil, vegetables, succotash and onion in a 6-quart saucepan to a boil over medium-high heat.

2 Reduce the heat to low. Cover the saucepan and cook for 45 minutes or until the vegetables are tender.

KITCHEN TIP

Stir in **1 cup** cooked pasta after the vegetables are cooked to make this a heartier soup.

ZESTY TACO SALAD

MAKES 4 SERVINGS

2 tablespoons canola oil

1 tablespoon red wine vinegar

1 clove garlic, minced

¾ pound ground turkey or ground beef

1¾ teaspoons chili powder

¼ teaspoon ground cumin

3 cups torn lettuce leaves

1 can (about 14 ounces) Mexican-style diced tomatoes, drained

1 cup canned chickpeas or pinto beans, rinsed and drained

⅔ cup chopped peeled cucumber

⅓ cup thawed frozen corn

¼ cup chopped red onion

1 to 2 jalapeño peppers,* seeded and finely chopped

Tortilla chips

Fresh cilantro (optional)

Jalapeño peppers can sting and irritate the skin, so wear rubber gloves when handling peppers and do not touch your eyes.

1 Whisk oil, vinegar and garlic in small bowl until well blended.

2 Combine turkey, chili powder and cumin in large nonstick skillet; cook over medium heat 5 minutes or until turkey is no longer pink, stirring to break up meat.

3 Combine turkey, lettuce, tomatoes, chickpeas, cucumber, corn, onion and jalapeño in large bowl. Add dressing; toss to coat. Serve with tortilla chips; garnish with cilantro.

SPLIT PEA SOUP

MAKES 6 SERVINGS

1 package (16 ounces) dried green or yellow split peas

7 cups water

1 pound smoked ham hocks *or* 4 ounces smoked sausage links, sliced and quartered

2 carrots, chopped

1 onion, chopped

¾ teaspoon salt

½ teaspoon dried basil

¼ teaspoon dried oregano

¼ teaspoon black pepper

1 Rinse split peas thoroughly in colander under cold running water; discard any debris or blemished peas.

2 Combine peas, water, ham hocks, carrots, onion, salt, basil, oregano and pepper in large saucepan; bring to a boil over high heat. Reduce heat to medium-low; simmer 1 hour 15 minutes or until peas are tender, stirring occasionally. Stir frequently near end of cooking to prevent soup from scorching.

3 Remove ham hocks to cutting board; let stand until cool enough to handle. Remove ham from hocks; chop meat and discard bones.

4 Place 3 cups soup in blender or food processor; blend until smooth. Return to saucepan; stir in ham. If soup is too thick, add water until desired consistency is reached. Cook just until heated through.

FRENCH ONION SOUP

MAKES 4 SERVINGS | PREP TIME 10 MINUTES **COOK TIME** 45 MINUTES

1 tablespoon vegetable oil

2½ large onions, halved and thinly sliced (about 2½ cups)*

¼ teaspoon sugar

2 tablespoons all-purpose flour

3½ cups SWANSON® Beef Broth (Regular, Lower Sodium *or* Certified Organic)

¼ cup dry white wine *or* vermouth

4 slices French bread, toasted**

½ cup shredded Swiss cheese (about 2 ounces)

Use a food processor with slicing attachment for ease in preparation.

**For even more flavor, try rubbing the bread with a garlic clove and topping it with the cheese before toasting.*

1 Heat the oil in a 4-quart saucepan over medium heat. Add the onions. Reduce the heat to low. Cover and cook for 15 minutes. Uncover the saucepan.

2 Increase the heat to medium. Add the sugar and cook for 15 minutes or until the onions are golden.

3 Stir the flour in the saucepan and cook and stir for 1 minute. Stir in the broth and wine. Heat to a boil. Reduce the heat to low. Cook for 10 minutes.

4 Divide the soup among **4** bowls. Top **each** with a bread slice and cheese.

TURKEY CLUB SALAD

MAKES 4 SERVINGS | PREP TIME 15 MINUTES

8 cups coarsely chopped romaine lettuce leaves

2 large hard-cooked eggs, diced

1 cup cherry tomatoes, halved

4 slices bacon, crisp-cooked and crumbled

1 container (4 ounces) blue cheese crumbles

8 slices deli turkey breast, rolled-up

½ cup WISH-BONE® Ranch Dressing

Arrange lettuce on large platter. Top with rows of eggs, tomatoes, bacon, cheese and turkey. Just before serving, drizzle with WISH-BONE® Ranch Dressing.

GREEK LEMON AND RICE SOUP

MAKES 6 TO 8 SERVINGS

2 tablespoons butter

⅓ cup minced green onions

6 cups chicken broth

⅔ cup uncooked long grain rice

4 eggs

Juice of 1 fresh lemon

⅛ teaspoon white pepper (optional)

Fresh mint and lemon peel (optional)

1 Melt butter in medium saucepan over medium heat. Add green onions; cook and stir about 3 minutes or until tender.

2 Stir in broth and rice; bring to a boil over medium-high heat. Reduce heat to low; cover and simmer 20 to 25 minutes or until rice is tender.

3 Beat eggs in medium bowl. Stir in lemon juice and ½ cup broth mixture until blended. Gradually pour egg mixture into broth mixture in saucepan, stirring constantly. Cook and stir over low heat 2 to 3 minutes or until soup thickens enough to lightly coat spoon. *Do not boil.*

4 Stir in pepper, if desired. Garnish with mint and lemon peel.

TOSSED GREEK SALAD WITH GRILLED SHRIMP

MAKES 6 SERVINGS

PREP TIME 15 MINUTES **MARINATE TIME** 30 MINUTES **COOK TIME** 5 MINUTES

¾ cup WISH-BONE® Robusto Italian or Italian Dressing, divided

1 pound uncooked medium shrimp, peeled and deveined

6 cups chopped romaine lettuce leaves

2 cups baby spinach leaves

1 medium seedless cucumber, peeled, halved lengthwise and sliced

1 large tomato, chopped

1 container (4 ounces) Mediterranean-style feta cheese crumbles*

Also terrific with plain feta cheese crumbles.

1 Pour ¼ cup WISH-BONE® Robusto Italian Dressing over shrimp in small nonaluminum baking dish or resealable plastic bag. Cover dish or close bag and marinate in refrigerator, turning occasionally, 30 minutes.

2 Remove shrimp from marinade, discarding marinade. Grill or broil shrimp 5 minutes or until shrimp turn pink, turning once.

3 Combine remaining ingredients in large serving bowl. Add shrimp and toss. Serve immediately.

VARIATION

Add fresh oregano to the dressing for more authentic Greek flavor.

CREAM OF BROCCOLI SOUP

MAKES 8 SERVINGS

3 cups French or rustic bread, cut into ½-inch cubes

3 tablespoons butter, melted, divided

1 tablespoon olive oil

¼ cup grated Parmesan cheese

1 large onion, chopped

8 cups (about 1½ pounds) chopped broccoli

3 cups chicken broth

1 cup whipping cream or half-and-half

1½ teaspoons salt

½ teaspoon black pepper

1 Preheat oven to 350°F. Combine bread cubes, 1 tablespoon butter and oil; toss to coat. Add cheese; toss again. Spread bread cubes on 15×10-inch jelly-roll pan.

2 Bake 12 to 14 minutes or until golden brown, stirring after 8 minutes. Cool completely; transfer to airtight container. (Croutons may be prepared up to 2 days before serving.)

3 Heat remaining 2 tablespoons butter in large saucepan over medium heat. Add onion; cook 5 minutes, stirring occasionally. Add broccoli and broth; bring to a boil over high heat. Reduce heat to low; simmer 25 minutes or until broccoli is very tender. Cool 10 minutes.

4 Blend soup in blender or food processor until smooth. Return to saucepan; stir in cream, salt and pepper. Cook over medium heat until heated through. *Do not boil.* Top with croutons.

NOTE

Soup may be cooled and refrigerated up to 2 days before serving.

COBB SALAD

MAKES 4 SERVINGS

1 package (10 ounces) torn mixed salad greens *or* 8 cups torn romaine lettuce

6 ounces cooked chicken breast, cut into bite-size pieces

1 tomato, seeded and chopped

2 hard-cooked eggs, cut into bite-size pieces

4 slices bacon, crisp-cooked and crumbled

1 ripe avocado, diced

1 large carrot, shredded

½ cup blue cheese, crumbled

Blue cheese dressing

Place lettuce in serving bowl. Arrange chicken, tomato, eggs, bacon, avocado, carrot and cheese over lettuce. Serve with dressing.

VEGETABLE-CHICKEN NOODLE SOUP

MAKES 6 SERVINGS

1 cup chopped celery

½ cup thinly sliced leek

½ cup chopped carrot

½ cup chopped turnip

6 cups chicken broth, divided

1 tablespoon minced fresh parsley

1½ teaspoons fresh thyme *or* ½ teaspoon dried thyme

1 teaspoon minced fresh rosemary leaves *or* ¼ teaspoon dried rosemary

1 teaspoon balsamic vinegar

¼ teaspoon black pepper

2 ounces uncooked wide egg noodles

1 cup diced cooked boneless skinless chicken breast

1 Combine celery, leek, carrot, turnip and ⅓ cup broth in large saucepan; cover and cook over medium heat 12 to 15 minutes or until vegetables are tender, stirring occasionally.

2 Stir in remaining 5⅔ cups broth, parsley, thyme, rosemary, vinegar and pepper; bring to a boil over medium-high heat. Stir in noodles; cook until noodles are tender.

3 Stir in chicken. Reduce heat to medium; cook until heated through.

MINESTRONE SOUP

MAKES 4 TO 6 SERVINGS

¾ cup uncooked small shell pasta

2 cans (about 14 ounces each) vegetable broth

1 can (28 ounces) crushed tomatoes in tomato purée

1 can (about 15 ounces) white beans, rinsed and drained

1 package (16 ounces) frozen vegetable medley, such as broccoli, green beans, carrots and red peppers

4 to 6 teaspoons prepared pesto

1 Cook pasta according to package directions; drain.

2 Meanwhile, combine broth, tomatoes and beans in large saucepan; bring to a boil over high heat. Reduce heat to low; cover and simmer 3 to 5 minutes.

3 Add vegetables to broth mixture; return to a boil over high heat. Stir in pasta; cook, uncovered, until vegetables and pasta are tender. Top each serving with about 1 teaspoon pesto.

TEX-MEX CHILI

MAKES 6 SERVINGS

4 slices bacon, diced

2 pounds boneless beef top round or chuck shoulder steak, trimmed and cut into ½-inch cubes

1 medium onion, chopped

2 cloves garlic, minced

¼ cup chili powder

1 teaspoon dried oregano

1 teaspoon salt

1 teaspoon ground cumin

½ to 1 teaspoon ground red pepper

½ teaspoon hot pepper sauce

4 cups water

Additional chopped onion (optional)

1 Cook bacon in large saucepan or Dutch oven over medium-high heat until crisp. Remove with slotted spoon; drain on paper towel-lined plate.

2 Add half of beef to bacon drippings in saucepan; cook and stir until lightly browned. Remove beef to plate; repeat with remaining beef.

3 Add onion and garlic to saucepan; cook and stir over medium heat until onion is tender. Return beef and bacon to saucepan. Stir in chili powder, oregano, salt, cumin, red pepper, hot pepper sauce and water; bring to a boil over high heat.

4 Reduce heat to low; cover and cook 1½ hours. Skim fat from surface; cook, uncovered, 30 minutes or until beef is very tender and chili has thickened slightly. Garnish with additional onion.

CLASSIC SANDWICHES

DINER EGG SALAD SANDWICHES

MAKES 4 SERVINGS

6 eggs

3 tablespoons mayonnaise

1½ tablespoons sweet pickle relish

½ cup finely chopped celery

¼ teaspoon salt

Black pepper

8 slices whole grain bread

1 Place eggs in medium saucepan; add cold water to cover. Bring to a boil over high heat. Reduce heat to low; simmer 10 minutes. Drain and peel eggs under cold running water.

2 Cut eggs in half. Set aside egg whites; place egg yolks in medium bowl. Add mayonnaise and pickle relish; mash with fork until yolk mixture is well blended and creamy.

3 Chop egg whites; add to yolk mixture with celery and salt. Stir until well blended. Season with pepper.

4 Spread ½ cup egg salad on each of 4 bread slices; top with remaining bread slices.

MEATBALL HERO SANDWICHES

MAKES 6 SERVINGS | PREP TIME 10 MINUTES **COOK TIME** 25 MINUTES

1½ pounds lean ground beef

½ cup Italian seasoned dry bread crumbs

1 egg

1 jar (1 pound 8 ounces) RAGÚ® Chunky Pasta Sauce

6 Italian rolls (about 6 inches long each), halved lengthwise

½ cup shredded part-skim mozzarella cheese (about 2 ounces)

1 Combine ground beef, bread crumbs and egg in medium bowl; shape into 18 meatballs.

2 Bring Pasta Sauce to a boil in 3-quart saucepan over medium-high heat. Gently stir in uncooked meatballs.

3 Reduce heat to low and simmer covered, stirring occasionally, 20 minutes or until meatballs are done. Serve meatballs and sauce in rolls and top with cheese.

TIP

Prepare extra meatball mixture and freeze it in individual portions. Then, for a last minute dinner, pull out and heat just what you need.

TUNA MONTE CRISTO SANDWICHES

MAKES 2 SERVINGS

4 slices (½ ounce each)
Cheddar cheese

4 slices sourdough or
challah (egg) bread

½ pound deli tuna salad

¼ cup milk

1 egg

2 tablespoons butter

1 Place 1 cheese slice on each of 2 bread slices. Spread tuna salad evenly over cheese; top with remaining cheese and bread slices.

2 Whisk milk and egg in shallow bowl until well blended. Dip sandwiches in egg mixture, turning to coat.

3 Melt butter in large nonstick skillet over medium heat. Add sandwiches; cook 4 to 5 minutes per side or until cheese melts and sandwiches are golden brown.

GREEK-STYLE STEAK SANDWICHES

MAKES 8 SANDWICHES

2 teaspoons Greek seasoning or dried oregano

1 beef flank steak (about 1½ pounds)

4 pita bread rounds, halved crosswise

1 small cucumber, thinly sliced

1 tomato, cut into thin wedges

½ cup sliced red onion

½ cup crumbled feta cheese

¼ cup red wine vinaigrette

1 cup plain yogurt

1 Rub Greek seasoning over both sides of steak. Place on plate; cover and refrigerate 30 to 60 minutes.

2 Prepare grill for direct cooking. Grill steak, covered, over medium-high heat 17 to 21 minutes or to desired doneness, turning once. Remove steak to cutting board. Tent with foil; let stand 10 minutes before slicing.

3 Meanwhile, grill pita halves about 1 minute per side or until warm. Slice steak into thin strips against the grain.

4 Divide steak among pita halves; top with cucumber, tomato, onion and cheese. Drizzle with vinaigrette; serve with yogurt.

CLASSIC SANDWICHES

GRILLED CHEESE, HAM & ONION MELTS
MAKES 4 SERVINGS | PREP TIME 10 MINUTES **COOK TIME** 30 MINUTES

1 tablespoon butter
   or margarine

2 medium onions,
   thinly sliced

1 teaspoon sugar

⅓ cup FRENCH'S® Honey
   Dijon Mustard

16 slices Muenster cheese

12 slices deli ham

 8 slices rye bread

1 Melt butter in medium nonstick skillet. Add onions. Cook over medium-high heat until tender, stirring often. Reduce heat to medium-low. Stir in sugar; cook 15 to 20 minutes or until onions are caramelized. Stir in mustard and remove from heat.

2 Place 2 slices cheese and 3 slices ham on each of 4 slices of bread. Spoon ¼ cup onion mixture over ham. Top with 2 more slices cheese and cover with remaining bread slices.

3 Coat an electric grill pan with nonstick cooking spray. Grill sandwiches about 5 minutes until golden and cheese melts.

TIP
Substitute deli roast beef for ham.

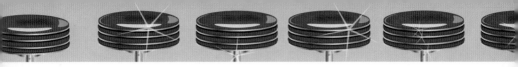

SHREDDED BBQ CHICKEN SANDWICHES

MAKES 8 SERVINGS | PREP TIME 10 MINUTES **COOK TIME** 25 MINUTES

2 jars (16 ounces each)
   PACE® Picante Sauce

1 tablespoon apple cider
   vinegar

¼ cup packed brown sugar

½ teaspoon garlic powder

¼ teaspoon chili powder

4 skinless, boneless
   chicken breast halves
   (about 1 pound)

1 package (13 ounces)
   PEPPERIDGE FARM®
   Classic Sandwich Buns
   with Sesame Seeds

Shredded Cheddar
   cheese

1 Heat the picante sauce, vinegar, brown sugar, garlic powder and chili powder in a 3-quart saucepan over medium-high heat to a boil.

2 Add the chicken to the saucepan. Reduce the heat to low. Cover and cook for 20 minutes or until the chicken is fork-tender.

3 Remove the chicken from the saucepan to a cutting board. Using 2 forks, shred the chicken. Return the chicken to the saucepan and cook until the mixture is hot and bubbling. Serve the chicken mixture on the buns. Sprinkle with the cheese.

CLASSIC SANDWICHES

GRILLED REUBENS WITH COLESLAW

MAKES 4 SERVINGS

2 cups sauerkraut

¼ cup (½ stick) butter, softened

8 slices marble rye or rye bread

12 ounces thinly sliced deli corned beef or pastrami

4 slices Swiss cheese

¼ to ½ cup prepared Thousand Island dressing

2 cups deli coleslaw

4 kosher garlic pickle spears

1 Preheat indoor grill or large grill pan. Drain sauerkraut well on paper towels.

2 Spread butter evenly over one side of each bread slice. Turn 4 bread slices over; layer with corned beef, sauerkraut and cheese. Top with remaining 4 bread slices, butter side up.

3 Grill sandwiches 2 minutes per side or just until cheese begins to melt. Spread 1 to 2 tablespoons dressing over corned beef. Serve with coleslaw and pickles.

TIP

Stack sandwich ingredients in the order listed to prevent sogginess.

PHILLY CHEESESTEAK SANDWICHES

MAKES 4 SANDWICHES | PREP TIME 10 MINUTES **COOK TIME** 25 MINUTES

1 box (1 pound 5 ounces) frozen thin beef sandwich steaks

1 tablespoon olive oil

2 large sweet onions, halved and thinly sliced

1 large red bell pepper, cut into ¼-inch strips

¼ teaspoon salt

⅛ teaspoon ground black pepper

1 jar (1 pound) RAGÚ® Cheesy! Double Cheddar Sauce

4 hoagie rolls, split

1 In 12-inch nonstick skillet, cook steaks, 2 at a time, over medium-high heat, stirring occasionally and breaking into pieces, 2 minutes or until done. Remove from skillet; set aside and keep warm. Repeat with remaining steaks. Clean skillet.

2 In same skillet, heat olive oil over medium heat and cook onions and red pepper, stirring occasionally, 15 minutes or until onions are caramelized. Season with salt and pepper.

3 Return steaks to skillet with ½ of the Double Cheddar Sauce. Cook, stirring occasionally, 2 minutes or until heated through.

4 To serve, evenly divide steak mixture among rolls, then drizzle with remaining Double Cheddar Sauce, heated.

CLASSIC SANDWICHES

SOUTHWESTERN SLOPPY JOES

MAKES 8 SERVINGS

1 pound ground beef

1 cup chopped onion

¼ cup chopped celery

¼ cup water

1 can (10 ounces) diced tomatoes with green chiles

1 can (8 ounces) tomato sauce

4 teaspoons packed brown sugar

½ teaspoon ground cumin

¼ teaspoon salt

8 whole wheat hamburger buns

1 Cook beef, onion, celery and water in large nonstick skillet over medium-high heat 6 to 8 minutes, stirring to break up meat. Drain fat.

2 Stir in tomatoes, tomato sauce, brown sugar, cumin and salt; bring to a boil over high heat. Reduce heat to low; cook 20 minutes or until mixture thickens. Spoon about ⅓ cup meat mixture onto each bun.

CREAMED TURKEY SANDWICH

MAKES 4 SERVINGS

1 tablespoon butter

½ cup chopped red bell pepper

½ cup sliced mushrooms

⅓ cup chopped green onions

1 can (about 10 ounces) cream of chicken soup

½ cup sour cream

⅓ cup milk

2 cups cubed cooked BUTTERBALL® Breast of Turkey

Prepared biscuits or toast

Chopped fresh parsley (optional)

1 Melt butter in large skillet over medium-high heat. Add bell pepper, mushrooms and green onions; cook and stir until tender.

2 Add soup, sour cream and milk; cook and stir until well blended and heated throughout. Stir in turkey.

3 Serve over warm biscuits or toast. Sprinkle with parsley, if desired.

GRILLED REUBEN BURGER

MAKES 6 SERVINGS

1½ pounds ground beef

½ cup water

½ cup shredded Swiss cheese (about 2 ounces)

1 envelope LIPTON® RECIPE SECRETS® Onion Soup Mix*

1 tablespoon crisp-cooked crumbled bacon or bacon bits

½ teaspoon caraway seeds (optional)

Also terrific with LIPTON® RECIPE SECRETS® Onion Mushroom Soup Mix.

1 In large bowl, combine all ingredients; shape into 6 patties.

2 Grill or broil until done. Top, if desired, with heated sauerkraut and additional bacon.

MAIN DISHES

SPAGHETTI AND MEATBALLS

MAKES 4 SERVINGS

8 ounces uncooked spaghetti

12 ounces ground beef

4 ounces hot Italian sausage, casing removed

1 egg white

2 tablespoons plain dry bread crumbs

1 teaspoon dried oregano

2 cups tomato-basil pasta sauce

3 tablespoons chopped fresh basil

2 tablespoons grated Parmesan cheese

1 Preheat oven to 450°F. Spray baking sheet with nonstick cooking spray. Cook spaghetti according to package directions; drain and keep warm.

2 Combine beef, sausage, egg white, bread crumbs and oregano in medium bowl; mix well. Shape into 16 (1½-inch) meatballs. Place on prepared baking sheet. Bake 12 minutes, turning once.

3 Pour pasta sauce into large skillet. Add meatballs; cook over medium heat 9 minutes or until sauce is heated through and meatballs are cooked through (160°F), stirring occasionally.

4 Divide spaghetti among 4 plates. Top with meatballs and sauce; sprinkle with basil and cheese.

YANKEE POT ROAST

MAKES 6 SERVINGS | PREP AND COOK TIME 3 TO 3½ HOURS

1 boneless beef chuck pot roast (arm, shoulder or blade), about 2½ pounds

⅓ cup all-purpose flour

¾ teaspoon salt

¾ teaspoon pepper

1 tablespoon vegetable oil

1 can (14 to 14½ ounces) beef broth

½ cup dry red wine

1½ teaspoons dried thyme leaves, crushed

2 packages (16 ounces *each*) frozen stew vegetable mixture (such as potatoes, carrots, celery and onion)

1 Combine flour, salt and pepper. Lightly coat beef in 2 tablespoons of the flour mixture. Heat oil in large stockpot over medium heat until hot. Place beef pot roast in stockpot; brown evenly. Pour off drippings.

2 Combine beef broth, red wine, thyme and remaining flour mixture; add to stockpot and bring to a boil. Reduce heat; cover tightly and simmer 2 hours. Add vegetables to stockpot; continue simmering 30 to 45 minutes or until pot roast and vegetables are fork-tender.

3 Remove pot roast and vegetables; keep warm. Skim fat from cooking liquid, if necessary.

4 Cut pot roast into bite-size pieces. Serve with vegetables and gravy.

Favorite recipe from **National Cattlemen's Beef Association on behalf of The Beef Checkoff**

OVEN-ROASTED BOSTON SCROD

MAKES 6 SERVINGS

½ cup seasoned dry bread crumbs

1 teaspoon grated lemon peel

1 teaspoon paprika

1 teaspoon dried dill weed

3 tablespoons all-purpose flour

2 egg whites

1 tablespoon water

1½ pounds Boston scrod or orange roughy fillets, cut into 6 pieces (4 ounces each)

2 tablespoons butter, melted

Tartar Sauce (recipe follows)

Lemon wedges

1 Preheat oven to 400°F. Spray 15×10-inch jelly-roll pan with nonstick cooking spray.

2 Combine bread crumbs, lemon peel, paprika and dill in shallow bowl or pie plate. Place flour in large resealable food storage bag. Beat egg whites and water in another shallow bowl or pie plate. Add fish, one fillet at a time, to flour. Seal bag; turn to coat. Remove fillet; dip into egg white mixture, letting excess drip off. Roll in bread crumb mixture to coat. Place on prepared pan; drizzle with butter.

3 Bake 15 to 18 minutes or until fish begins to flake when tested with fork.

4 Meanwhile, prepare Tartar Sauce. Serve fish with Tartar Sauce and lemon wedges.

TARTAR SAUCE

Combine ½ cup mayonnaise, ¼ cup sweet pickle relish, 2 teaspoons Dijon mustard and ¼ teaspoon hot pepper sauce, if desired, in small bowl; mix well.

MAIN DISHES

BEEF STROGANOFF

MAKES 4 SERVINGS | PREP TIME 10 MINUTES **COOK TIME** 25 MINUTES

1 tablespoon vegetable oil

1 boneless beef sirloin steak *or* beef top round steak, ¾-inch thick (about 1 pound), cut into thin strips

1 medium onion, chopped (about ½ cup)

1 can (10¾ ounces) CAMPBELL'S® Condensed Cream of Mushroom Soup (Regular, 98% Fat Free *or* Healthy Request®)

½ teaspoon paprika

⅓ cup sour cream *or* plain yogurt

4 cups whole wheat *or* regular egg noodles, cooked and drained

Chopped fresh parsley

1 Heat the oil in a 12-inch nonstick skillet over medium-high heat. Add the beef and cook until well browned, stirring often. Remove the beef from the skillet. Pour off any fat.

2 Reduce the heat to medium. Add the onion to the skillet and cook until tender.

3 Stir the soup and paprika in the skillet and heat to a boil. Stir in the sour cream. Return the beef to the skillet and cook until the beef is cooked through. Serve the beef mixture over the noodles. Sprinkle with the parsley.

SERVING SUGGESTION

Serve with sautéed spinach with garlic and crusty French bread. For dessert serve a fresh apple and raisin cup: cubed, cored apples mixed with raisins.

MAIN DISHES

PEPPERED PORK CUTLETS WITH ONION GRAVY

MAKES 4 SERVINGS

½ teaspoon paprika

¼ teaspoon ground cumin

¼ teaspoon black pepper

⅛ teaspoon ground red pepper (optional)

4 boneless pork cutlets (4 ounces each)

1 tablespoon vegetable oil

2 cups thinly sliced onions

2 tablespoons all-purpose flour, divided

¾ cup water

1½ teaspoons chicken bouillon granules

2 tablespoons milk

¼ teaspoon salt

1 Combine paprika, cumin, black pepper and red pepper, if desired in small bowl; mix well. Sprinkle evenly over one side of each cutlet; press down gently. Let stand 15 minutes.

2 Heat oil in large skillet over medium heat. Add pork, seasoned side down; cook 3 minutes or until browned. Remove to plate. Add onions to skillet; cook and stir over medium-high heat 3 to 5 minutes or until browned. Add 1½ tablespoons flour; stir until well blended. Stir in water and bouillon; bring to a boil.

3 Return pork and any accumulated juices to skillet; spoon sauce over pork. Reduce heat to low; cover and cook 15 to 20 minutes or until pork is barely pink in center.

4 Remove pork to plate; cover to keep warm. Stir milk and salt into onion mixture in skillet; cook 1 to 2 minutes. Serve pork with onion gravy.

OVEN-FRIED CHICKEN

MAKES 4 SERVINGS

1⅓ cups light-colored beer, such as pale ale

2 tablespoons buttermilk

1¼ cups panko bread crumbs

½ cup grated Parmesan cheese

4 chicken breast cutlets (about 1¼ pounds)

½ teaspoon salt

¼ teaspoon black pepper

1 Preheat oven to 400°F. Line large baking sheet with foil.

2 Combine beer and buttermilk in shallow bowl. Combine panko and cheese in another shallow bowl.

3 Sprinkle chicken with salt and pepper. Dip in beer mixture; roll in panko mixture to coat. Place on prepared baking sheet.

4 Bake 25 to 30 minutes or until chicken is no longer pink in center.

TIP

If you don't have buttermilk, place ¾ teaspoon lemon juice or white vinegar in a measuring cup and add enough milk to measure ¼ cup. Stir, then let the mixture stand at room temperature for 5 minutes. Discard the leftover mixture.

SMOTHERED PATTIES WITH ONION AU JUS

MAKES 4 SERVINGS

1 pound ground sirloin

¼ teaspoon salt

1 tablespoon vegetable oil, divided

1 medium onion, thinly sliced

¾ cup water

2 teaspoons beef bouillon granules

1 teaspoon Worcestershire sauce

½ teaspoon decaffeinated or regular instant coffee granules

⅛ teaspoon black pepper

1 Shape beef into 4 patties about 4 inches in diameter and ½ inch thick. Sprinkle with salt.

2 Heat 2 teaspoons oil in large nonstick skillet over medium-high heat. Add patties; cook 3 minutes per side or until just barely pink in center. Remove to plate.

3 Add remaining 1 teaspoon oil to skillet; heat over medium-high heat. Add onion; cook and stir 3 minutes or until tender. Transfer to plate. Add water, bouillon granules, Worcestershire sauce, coffee granules and pepper to skillet; bring to a boil. Reduce heat to medium-low; simmer 3 minutes or until mixture is reduced to about ½ cup.

4 Return patties and onion to skillet; turn patties several times to coat. Cook 1 minute or until heated through.

SHRIMP SCAMPI

MAKES 4 TO 6 SERVINGS

⅓ cup clarified butter*

2 to 4 tablespoons minced garlic

1½ pounds large raw shrimp, peeled and deveined (with tails on)

6 green onions, thinly sliced

¼ cup dry white wine

2 tablespoons lemon juice

Chopped fresh Italian parsley

Salt and black pepper

Lemon wedges

*To clarify butter, melt butter in small saucepan over low heat. Skim off white foam that forms on top, then strain remaining butter through cheesecloth. Discard cheesecloth and milky residue in bottom of pan. Clarified butter can be stored in airtight container in refrigerator up to 2 months.

1 Heat butter in large skillet over medium heat. Add garlic; cook and stir 1 to 2 minutes or until softened but not brown. Add shrimp, green onions, wine and lemon juice; cook 2 to 4 minutes or until shrimp are pink and opaque, stirring occasionally.

2 Sprinkle with parsley; season with salt and pepper. Serve with lemon wedges.

MEATLOAF

MAKES 4 SERVINGS | PREP TIME 15 MINUTES **START TO FINISH TIME** 1 HOUR 5 MINUTES

1 pound lean ground beef

1 egg, beaten

½ cup CREAM OF WHEAT® Hot Cereal (Instant, 1-minute, 2½-minute or 10-minute cook time), uncooked

¼ cup ketchup, divided

¼ cup finely chopped onion

2 tablespoons water

¾ teaspoon salt

1 Preheat oven to 350°F. Grease shallow baking dish.

2 Mix ground beef, egg, Cream of Wheat, 2 tablespoons ketchup, onion, water and salt in large bowl. Shape into loaf in prepared baking dish.

3 Bake 35 minutes. Spread remaining ketchup over meatloaf. Bake 15 minutes longer or until meat thermometer inserted into center reads 160°F.

TIP

Meatloaf can also be made with ground turkey. For a nutritious meal, serve with healthy side dishes, such as a whole-grain roll and steamed mixed vegetables.

ZESTY SKILLET PORK CHOPS

MAKES 4 SERVINGS

1 teaspoon chili powder

½ teaspoon salt, divided

4 boneless pork chops (about 1¼ pounds)

2 cups diced tomatoes

1 cup chopped green, red or yellow bell pepper

¾ cup thinly sliced celery

½ cup chopped onion

1 tablespoon hot pepper sauce

1 teaspoon dried thyme

1 tablespoon olive oil

2 tablespoons finely chopped parsley

1 Rub chili powder and ¼ teaspoon salt over one side of pork chops.

2 Combine tomatoes, bell pepper, celery, onion, hot pepper sauce and thyme in medium bowl; mix well.

3 Heat oil in large nonstick skillet over medium-high heat. Add pork, seasoned side down; cook 1 minute. Turn pork and top with tomato mixture; bring to a boil. Reduce heat to low; cover and cook 25 minutes or until pork is tender and tomato mixture has thickened.

4 Transfer pork to serving plates; cover to keep warm. Bring tomato mixture to a boil over high heat; cook 2 minutes or until most of liquid has evaporated. Remove from heat; stir in parsley and remaining ¼ teaspoon salt. Spoon sauce over pork.

BROILED CAJUN FISH FILLETS

MAKES 4 SERVINGS

2 tablespoons all-purpose flour

½ cup seasoned dry bread crumbs

1 teaspoon dried thyme

½ teaspoon garlic salt

¼ teaspoon ground red pepper

¼ teaspoon black pepper

1 egg

1 tablespoon milk or water

4 scrod or orange roughy fillets, ½ inch thick (4 to 5 ounces each)

2 tablespoons butter, melted, divided

⅓ cup mayonnaise

2 tablespoons sweet pickle relish

1 tablespoon lemon juice

1 teaspoon prepared horseradish

1 Preheat broiler. Spray baking sheet with nonstick cooking spray.

2 Place flour in large resealable food storage bag. Combine bread crumbs, thyme, garlic salt, red pepper and black pepper in second bag. Beat egg and milk in shallow dish. Working with one fillet at a time, place fillet in flour; shake bag to coat lightly. Dip fillet in egg mixture, letting excess drip off. Place fillet in bread crumb mixture; shake to coat. Place on prepared baking sheet; brush with 1 tablespoon butter.

3 Broil 4 to 5 inches from heat 3 minutes. Turn fish; brush with remaining 1 tablespoon butter. Broil 3 minutes or until fish begins to flake when tested with fork.

4 Meanwhile, combine mayonnaise, relish, juice and horseradish in small bowl; mix well. Serve sauce with fish.

LONDON BROIL WITH MARINATED VEGETABLES

MAKES 6 SERVINGS

¾ cup olive oil

¾ cup dry red wine

2 tablespoons red wine vinegar

2 tablespoons finely chopped shallots

2 teaspoons minced garlic

½ teaspoon dried thyme

½ teaspoon dried oregano

½ teaspoon dried basil

½ teaspoon black pepper

2 pounds top round London broil (1½ inches thick)

1 medium red onion, cut into ¼-inch-thick slices

1 package (8 ounces) sliced mushrooms

1 medium red bell pepper, cut into strips

1 medium zucchini, cut into ¼-inch-thick slices

1 Whisk oil, wine, vinegar, shallots, garlic, thyme, oregano, basil and black pepper in medium bowl until well blended. Combine London broil and ¾ cup marinade in large resealable food storage bag. Seal bag; turn to coat. Marinate in refrigerator up to 24 hours, turning bag once or twice.

2 Combine onion, mushrooms, bell pepper, zucchini and remaining marinade in separate large food storage bag. Seal bag; turn to coat. Marinate in refrigerator up to 24 hours, turning bag once or twice.

3 Preheat broiler. Remove beef from marinade and place on broiler pan; discard marinade. Broil 4 to 5 inches from heat about 9 minutes per side or until desired doneness. Let stand 10 minutes before slicing. Cut beef into thin slices.

4 Meanwhile, drain vegetables and arrange on broiler pan; discard marinade. Broil 4 to 5 inches from heat about 9 minutes or until edges of vegetables just begin to brown. Serve vegetables with beef.

MAIN DISHES

DINER DESSERTS

CLASSIC APPLE PIE
MAKES 8 SERVINGS

1 package (15 ounces) refrigerated pie crusts

6 cups sliced Granny Smith, Crispin or other firm-fleshed apples (about 6 medium)

½ cup sugar

1 tablespoon cornstarch

2 teaspoons lemon juice

½ teaspoon ground cinnamon

½ teaspoon vanilla

⅛ teaspoon salt

⅛ teaspoon ground nutmeg

⅛ teaspoon ground cloves

1 tablespoon whipping cream

1 Let one crust stand at room temperature 15 minutes. Preheat oven to 350°F. Line 9-inch pie plate with crust.

2 Combine apples, sugar, cornstarch, lemon juice, cinnamon, vanilla, salt, nutmeg and cloves in large bowl; mix well. Pour into crust. Place second crust over apples; crimp edge to seal. Cut 4 slits in top crust; brush with cream.

3 Bake 40 minutes or until crust is golden brown. Cool completely on wire rack.

OLD-FASHIONED DEVIL'S FOOD CAKE

MAKES 12 TO 16 SERVINGS

6 tablespoons (¾ stick) butter, softened

1½ cups granulated sugar

3 eggs

1½ teaspoons vanilla

2 cups cake flour

½ cup unsweetened cocoa powder

2 teaspoons baking powder

½ teaspoon baking soda

½ teaspoon salt

1 cup buttermilk*

Creamy Chocolate Frosting (recipe follows)

If buttermilk is unavailable, substitute 1 tablespoon vinegar or lemon juice and enough milk to equal 1 cup. Stir; let stand 5 minutes.

1 Preheat oven to 350°F. Grease and flour 3 (8-inch) round cake pans.

2 Beat butter and granulated sugar in large bowl with electric mixer at medium speed until fluffy. Beat in eggs and vanilla until blended.

3 Combine flour, cocoa, baking powder, baking soda and salt in medium bowl; mix well. Add to butter mixture alternately with buttermilk, beating well after each addition. Pour batter evenly into prepared pans.

4 Bake 25 to 30 minutes or until toothpick inserted into centers comes out clean. Cool in pans 10 minutes; remove to wire racks to cool completely.

5 Meanwhile, prepare Creamy Chocolate Frosting. Place one cake layer on serving plate; spread with frosting. Repeat with remaining cake layers and frosting. Frost side and top of cake.

CREAMY CHOCOLATE FROSTING

Beat 6 tablespoons (¾ stick) softenend butter in large bowl with electric mixer at medium speed until creamy. Gradually add 5 cups powdered sugar and ½ cup unsweetened cocoa powder, beating until smooth. Add 6 tablespoons milk and 1 teaspoon vanilla; beat until desired consistency is reached.

DINER DESSERTS

NECTARINE-RASPBERRY COBBLER

MAKES 6 SERVINGS

3 cups sliced peeled nectarines or peaches (about 1¼ pounds)

½ cup fresh raspberries

3 tablespoons sugar, divided

1 tablespoon cornstarch

½ teaspoon ground cinnamon

¾ cup all-purpose flour

1 teaspoon grated lemon peel

¾ teaspoon baking powder

¼ teaspoon salt

⅛ teaspoon baking soda

3 tablespoons cold butter, cut into small pieces

½ cup buttermilk

1 Preheat oven to 375°F.

2 Combine nectarines and raspberries in large bowl. Combine 2 tablespoons sugar, cornstarch and cinnamon in small bowl; mix well. Add to fruit; toss gently to coat. Spoon into 8-inch round baking dish.

3 Combine flour, lemon peel, baking powder, salt, baking soda and remaining 1 tablespoon sugar in medium bowl. Cut in butter with pastry blender or two knives until mixture resembles coarse crumbs. Stir in buttermilk until blended. Drop dough in 6 equal spoonfuls over fruit.

4 Bake 25 to 27 minutes or until filling is bubbly and topping is just beginning to brown. Serve warm.

NOTE

One pound of frozen unsweetened peach slices and ½ cup frozen unsweetened raspberries may be substituted for the fresh fruit. Let the peach slices stand at room temperature until almost thawed, at least 2 hours. Use the raspberries frozen. Bake an additional 3 to 5 minutes or until the filling is bubbly and the topping is beginning to brown.

DEEP-DISH BLUEBERRY PIE
MAKES 8 SERVINGS

Double-Crust Pie Pastry
(recipe follows)

6 cups fresh blueberries *or*
2 (16-ounce) packages
frozen blueberries,
thawed and drained

2 tablespoons lemon juice

1¼ cups sugar

3 tablespoons quick-
cooking tapioca

¼ teaspoon ground
cinnamon

1 tablespoon butter, cut
into small pieces

1 Prepare Double-Crust Pie Pastry. Preheat oven to 400°F.

2 Place blueberries in large bowl; sprinkle with lemon juice.
Combine sugar, tapioca and cinnamon in small bowl; mix
well. Add to blueberries; stir gently until blended.

3 Roll one pastry disc into 12-inch circle on lightly floured surface.
Line 9-inch deep-dish pie plate with pastry; trim all but ½ inch of
overhang. Pour blueberry mixture into crust; dot with butter.

4 Roll out remaining pastry disc into 10-inch circle. Cut 4 or
5 shapes from dough with small cookie cutter or knife. Arrange
pastry over blueberry mixture; trim edge, leaving 1-inch border.
Fold excess pastry under and even with edge of pie plate.
Crimp edge with fork.

5 Bake 15 minutes. *Reduce oven temperature to 350°F.* Bake
40 minutes or until crust is golden brown. Cool on wire rack
30 minutes.

DOUBLE-CRUST PIE PASTRY

Combine 2½ cups all-purpose flour, 1 teaspoon salt and
1 teaspoon sugar in large bowl. Cut in 1 cup (2 sticks) cold
cubed butter with pastry blender or two knives until mixture
resembles coarse crumbs. Drizzle ⅓ cup ice water over flour
mixture, 2 tablespoons at a time, stirring just until dough
comes together. Divide dough in half. Shape each half into
a disc; wrap with plastic wrap. Refrigerate 30 minutes.

CHOCOLATE MARBLE PRALINE CHEESECAKE

MAKES 12 TO 16 SERVINGS

CRUST

1½ cups vanilla wafer crumbs

¼ cup powdered sugar

¼ cup (½ stick) butter, melted

½ cup finely chopped toasted pecans*

FILLING

1¼ cups packed brown sugar

2 tablespoons all-purpose flour

3 packages (8 ounces each) cream cheese, softened

3 eggs, lightly beaten

1½ teaspoons vanilla

1 ounce unsweetened chocolate, melted

20 to 25 pecan halves (½ cup)

Caramel ice cream topping

To toast pecans, spread on baking sheet. Bake in preheated 350°F oven 6 to 8 minutes or until lightly browned, stirring occasionally.

1 Preheat oven to 350°F.

2 For crust, combine wafer crumbs, powdered sugar, butter and chopped pecans in large bowl; mix well. Press mixture onto bottom and up side of ungreased 9-inch springform pan. Bake 10 to 15 minutes or until lightly browned.

3 For filling, combine brown sugar and flour in small bowl; mix well. Beat cream cheese in large bowl with electric mixer at low speed until fluffy; gradually add brown sugar mixture. Add eggs and vanilla; beat just until blended. Remove 1 cup batter to small bowl; stir in chocolate. Pour remaining plain batter over warm crust. Drop spoonfuls of chocolate batter over plain batter; run knife through batters to marbleize. Arrange pecan halves around edge.

4 Bake 45 to 55 minutes or until set. Loosen cake from side of pan. Cool completely on wire rack. Refrigerate 2 hours or until ready to serve.

5 Remove side of pan. Drizzle with caramel topping.

CLASSIC MINUTE RICE PUDDING

MAKES 4 SERVINGS

3 cups milk

1 cup MINUTE® White Rice, uncooked

¼ cup sugar

¼ cup raisins

¼ teaspoon salt

2 eggs

1 teaspoon vanilla

Combine milk, rice, sugar, raisins and salt in medium saucepan. Bring to a boil, stirring constantly. Reduce heat to medium-low; simmer 6 minutes, stirring occasionally.

Beat eggs and vanilla lightly in small bowl. Stir small amount of hot mixture into eggs. Stirring constantly, slowly pour egg mixture back into hot mixture.

Cook on low heat 1 minute, stirring constantly, until thickened. DO NOT BOIL. Remove from heat. Let stand 30 minutes.

Serve warm. Store any remaining pudding in refrigerator.

TIP

Create flavorful new varieties of rice puddings by trying different types of dried fruits instead of raisins, such as dried cherries, chopped dried apricots, chopped dried pineapple or sweetened dried cranberries.

STRAWBERRY SHORTCAKE

MAKES 6 SERVINGS | PREP TIME 10 MINUTES **COOK TIME** 5 MINUTES

½ cup orange juice

1 tablespoon cornstarch

1 package (14 ounces) DOLE® Frozen Sliced Strawberries (2 cups), partially thawed

¼ cup sugar

1 tablespoon orange marmalade

6 prepared biscuits

Prepared sweetened whipped cream or aerosol whipped cream

• **STIR** orange juice into cornstarch in medium saucepan. Add strawberries, sugar and marmalade. Bring to a boil, stirring occasionally. Reduce heat to low; cook 2 minutes, stirring, or until sauce thickens. Cool or chill.

• **SPLIT** open prepared biscuits. Spoon strawberry glaze over biscuits. Add spoonful whipped cream and biscuit top. Spoon additional glaze and strawberries over biscuits.

CREAMY COCONUT CAKE WITH ALMOND FILLING

MAKES 8 TO 12 SERVINGS

1 package (about 15 ounces) white cake mix

1 cup sour cream

3 eggs

½ cup vegetable oil

1 teaspoon vanilla

1 teaspoon coconut extract

1 can (12½ ounces) almond filling

2 containers (16 ounces each) creamy coconut frosting

½ cup sliced almonds

1 Preheat oven to 350°F. Grease and flour 2 (9-inch) round baking pans.

2 Beat cake mix, sour cream, eggs, oil, vanilla and coconut extract in large bowl with electric mixer at low speed 3 minutes or until well blended. Pour batter evenly into prepared pans.

3 Bake 30 to 35 minutes or until toothpicks inserted into centers come out clean. Cool completely in pans on wire racks.

4 Remove cake layers from pans; cut each layer in half horizontally to make 4 layers. Place one cake layer on serving plate; spread with half of almond filling. Top with second cake layer; spread with ½ cup coconut frosting. Top with third cake layer; spread with remaining almond filling. Top with fourth cake layer; spread remaining coconut frosting over top and side of cake. Sprinkle with almonds.

CHOCOLATE CHESS PIE
MAKES 8 SERVINGS

4 ounces unsweetened chocolate

3 tablespoons butter

3 eggs

1 egg yolk

1¼ cups sugar

½ cup half-and-half

1 to 2 teaspoons instant coffee granules

¼ teaspoon salt

1 unbaked 9-inch pie crust

Whipped cream

Chocolate-covered coffee beans (optional)

1 Preheat oven to 325°F.

2 Combine chocolate and butter in small heavy saucepan; heat over low heat until melted, stirring frequently. Let stand 15 minutes.

3 Whisk eggs and egg yolk in medium bowl. Whisk in sugar, half-and-half, coffee granules and salt until blended. Whisk in chocolate mixture until smooth. Pour into crust.

4 Bake 35 minutes or until set. Cool completely on wire rack. Refrigerate 2 hours or until ready to serve. Serve with whipped cream; garnish with chocolate-covered coffee beans.

ROOT BEER BARREL SHAKE

MAKES 1 SERVING

1 scoop vanilla ice cream
  or frozen yogurt

1 cup root beer

½ teaspoon root beer
  extract

Whipped cream

Root beer-flavored
  hard candy, crushed
  (optional)

1 Place glass mug in freezer at least 1 hour (or longer) before serving time, if desired.

2 Combine ice cream, root beer and root beer extract in blender; blend about 10 seconds or until smooth. Pour in frozen mug or glass. Top with whipped cream and candy, if desired.

NOTE

Root beer extract can be found in the baking aisle with the spices, extracts and flavorings.

CHOCOLATE CHERRY MILKSHAKE

MAKES 2 (10-OUNCE) SERVINGS

4 scoops (about 2 cups) vanilla ice cream or frozen yogurt

¾ cup cold milk

¼ cup HERSHEY'S® Syrup

8 maraschino cherries, stems removed

Whipped topping and additional cherries (optional)

1 Place ice cream, milk, chocolate syrup and cherries in blender container. Cover; blend until smooth.

2 Garnish with whipped topping and additional cherries, if desired.

CREAMY CHOCOLATE PUDDING

MAKES ABOUT 4 (½-CUP) SERVINGS
PREP TIME 5 MINUTES **COOK TIME** 7 MINUTES

6 tablespoons granulated sugar

¼ cup NESTLÉ® TOLL HOUSE® Baking Cocoa

¼ cup cornstarch

⅛ teaspoon salt

1 can (12 fluid ounces) NESTLÉ® CARNATION® Evaporated Fat Free Milk

½ cup water

1 tablespoon butter or margarine

½ teaspoon vanilla extract

COMBINE sugar, cocoa, cornstarch and salt in medium saucepan. Add evaporated milk and water; whisk to blend.

COOK over medium heat, stirring constantly, for about 7 minutes or until pudding thickens. Do not boil. Remove from heat; stir in butter and vanilla extract.

TART CHERRY PIE

MAKES 8 SERVINGS

Double-Crust Pie Pastry (recipe follows)

2 cans (about 14 ounces each) tart cherries, packed in water

1½ cups granulated sugar

¼ cup quick-cooking tapioca

1 teaspoon ground cinnamon

1 teaspoon grated lemon peel

2 tablespoons butter, cut into small pieces

1 egg beaten with 1 teaspoon water

Coarse sugar

1 Prepare Double-Crust Pie Pastry.

2 Preheat oven to 425°F. Drain cherries, reserving ½ cup juice. Place cherries and reserved juice in large bowl. Combine granulated sugar, tapioca, cinnamon and lemon peel in small bowl; mix well. Gently stir mixture into cherries.

3 Roll out one pastry disc into 12-inch circle on floured surface. Line 9-inch pie pan with pastry. Roll out remaining pastry disc into 11-inch circle on floured surface. Make slits in pastry with sharp knife.

4 Pour cherry mixture into crust; dot with butter. Top with second crust, folding edge under. Seal and flute edge. Brush crust lightly with egg mixture; sprinkle with coarse sugar. Place pie on baking sheet.

5 Bake 15 minutes. *Reduce oven temperature to 350°F.* Bake 30 to 35 minutes or until crust is brown and juices are bubbly. If necessary, cover pie loosely with foil during last 10 minutes of baking to prevent overbrowning. Cool on wire rack. Serve warm or at room temperature.

DOUBLE-CRUST PIE PASTRY

Combine 2 cups all-purpose flour and 1 teaspoon salt in medium bowl. Cut in 6 tablespoons cold cubed shortening and ¼ cup (½ stick) cold cubed butter with pastry blender or two knives until mixture resembles coarse crumbs. Combine 4 tablespoons ice water and ½ teaspoon cider vinegar in small bowl. Add to flour mixture; mix with fork until dough forms, adding additional water as needed. Divide dough in half. Shape each half into a disc; wrap with plastic wrap. Refrigerate 1 hour.

BANANA CAKE

MAKES 12 TO 16 SERVINGS

2½ cups all-purpose flour

1 tablespoon baking soda

½ teaspoon salt

1 cup granulated sugar

¾ cup packed brown sugar

½ cup (1 stick) butter, softened

2 eggs

1 teaspoon vanilla

3 ripe bananas, mashed (about 1⅔ cups)

⅔ cup buttermilk

1 container (16 ounces) dark chocolate frosting

1 Preheat oven to 350°F. Spray 2 (8-inch) round cake pans with nonstick cooking spray.

2 Combine flour, baking soda and salt in medium bowl; mix well. Beat granulated sugar, brown sugar and butter in large bowl with electric mixer at medium speed until well blended. Add eggs and vanilla; beat until blended. Stir in bananas. Alternately add flour mixture and buttermilk; beat until well blended after each addition. Pour batter evenly into prepared pans.

3 Bake 35 minutes or until toothpick inserted into centers comes out clean. Cool in pans 10 minutes; remove to wire racks to cool completely.

4 Fill and frost cake with chocolate frosting.

CITRUS TAPIOCA PUDDING
MAKES 8 SERVINGS

2 navel oranges

2½ cups milk

⅓ cup sugar

3 tablespoons quick-cooking
tapioca

1 egg, beaten

½ teaspoon almond extract

Ground cinnamon
or nutmeg

Additional orange slices
(optional)

1 Grate peel of 1 orange into medium saucepan. Stir in milk,
sugar, tapioca and egg; let stand 5 minutes.

2 Bring mixture to a boil over medium heat, stirring constantly.
Remove from heat; stir in almond extract. Let stand 20 minutes.
Stir pudding; cool to room temperature. Cover and refrigerate
at least 2 hours.

3 Peel and dice oranges. Stir pudding; gently fold in oranges.
Sprinkle with cinnamon; garnish with additional orange slices.

DINER DESSERTS

INDEX

INDEX

ACKNOWLEDGMENTS

The publisher would like to thank the companies and organizations listed below for the use of their recipes and photographs in this publication.

The Beef Checkoff

Bob Evans®

Butterball® Turkey

Campbell Soup Company

Cream of Wheat® Cereal, A Division of
B&G Foods North America, Inc.

Dole Food Company, Inc.

The Hershey Company

Nestlé USA

Pinnacle Foods

Reckitt Benckiser LLC

Riviana Foods Inc.

Unilever

METRIC CONVERSION CHART

VOLUME MEASUREMENTS (dry)

1/8 teaspoon = 0.5 mL
1/4 teaspoon = 1 mL
1/2 teaspoon = 2 mL
3/4 teaspoon = 4 mL
1 teaspoon = 5 mL
1 tablespoon = 15 mL
2 tablespoons = 30 mL
1/4 cup = 60 mL
1/3 cup = 75 mL
1/2 cup = 125 mL
2/3 cup = 150 mL
3/4 cup = 175 mL
1 cup = 250 mL
2 cups = 1 pint = 500 mL
3 cups = 750 mL
4 cups = 1 quart = 1 L

VOLUME MEASUREMENTS (fluid)

1 fluid ounce (2 tablespoons) = 30 mL
4 fluid ounces (1/2 cup) = 125 mL
8 fluid ounces (1 cup) = 250 mL
12 fluid ounces (1 1/2 cups) = 375 mL
16 fluid ounces (2 cups) = 500 mL

WEIGHTS (mass)

1/2 ounce = 15 g
1 ounce = 30 g
3 ounces = 90 g
4 ounces = 120 g
8 ounces = 225 g
10 ounces = 285 g
12 ounces = 360 g
16 ounces = 1 pound = 450 g

DIMENSIONS

1/16 inch = 2 mm
1/8 inch = 3 mm
1/4 inch = 6 mm
1/2 inch = 1.5 cm
3/4 inch = 2 cm
1 inch = 2.5 cm

OVEN TEMPERATURES

250°F = 120°C
275°F = 140°C
300°F = 150°C
325°F = 160°C
350°F = 180°C
375°F = 190°C
400°F = 200°C
425°F = 220°C
450°F = 230°C

BAKING PAN SIZES

Utensil	Size in Inches/Quarts	Metric Volume	Size in Centimeters
Baking or Cake Pan (square or rectangular)	8×8×2	2 L	20×20×5
	9×9×2	2.5 L	23×23×5
	12×8×2	3 L	30×20×5
	13×9×2	3.5 L	33×23×5
Loaf Pan	8×4×3	1.5 L	20×10×7
	9×5×3	2 L	23×13×7
Round Layer Cake Pan	8×1½	1.2 L	20×4
	9×1½	1.5 L	23×4
Pie Plate	8×1¼	750 mL	20×3
	9×1¼	1 L	23×3
Baking Dish or Casserole	1 quart	1 L	—
	1½ quart	1.5 L	—
	2 quart	2 L	—